WOODLAND
Lullabies

Joan Elizabeth Goodman

The Millbrook Press   Brookfield, Connecticut

To Henry Michael Goldsmith, my sweet inspiration

Library of Congress Cataloging-in-Publication Data
Goodman, Joan E.
Woodland lullabies / by Joan Elizabeth Goodman.
p. cm.
Summary: In each lullaby in this collection an animal parent
gently soothes its baby to prepare it for sleep.
ISBN 0-7613-0350-2 (lib. bdg.)
1. Animals—Juvenile poetry. 2. Children's poetry, American.
3. Lullabies, American. [1. Parent and child—Poetry. 2. Sleep—poetry.
3. Animals—Poetry. 4. Lullabies. 5. American poetry.] I. Title.
PS3557.O58376W66   1998
811'.54—dc21   97-35576   CIP   AC
Copyright © 1998 by Joan Elizabeth Goodman

Published by The Millbrook Press, Inc.
2 Old New Milford Road, Brookfield, CT 06804
5   4   3   2   1

Dawn

In den and nest and burrow
as Winter melts away,
new children of the Woodland
are arriving every day.

Hear parents sing their praises.
Hear them croon a lullaby.
Listen to the Woodland songs
that soothe a baby's cry.

The Vixen's Song

arly this morn
my cubs were born.
Six little fox cubs—
eyes closed,
snub nosed,
furred in brown
soft as down,
and dark
as bark.
Six little fox cubs
born this morn.
Six little cubs were born.

The Mole's Song

Hush, little molekins.
Sleep, go to sleep.
Safe in the musky deep,
down under the ground.
Safe from the stoat,
safe from the hound.
Let the quiet earth hold you
and the warm nest enfold you.
Hush, little molekins.
Sleep, go to sleep.
Follow the song down
deep . . . deep . . . deep
into the tunnels of fur-lined sleep.
Hush, my molekins.
Sleep, go to sleep.

The Owl's Song

hoo will ye be?
Whoo will ye be?
Owlets divine.
Owlets of mine.
Whoo will ye be
when you've flown
far from me?
Whoo will ye be
when you're grown?

The Bear's Song

I swear by my fur,
by my shaggy old fur,
there's none can compare
with my pair
of brown baby bears.
Sleep on, little brothers,
twined in each other's arms.
Sleep on through the night
sheltered from winter's storms.
Sleep 'til you're warmed
by spring's tender light.

The Rabbit's Song

Tomorrow there'll be clover.
There'll be frolics in the grass.
Now sleep, darling bunnies,
until the night shall pass.

Come summer you'll find carrots,
tasty peas within each pod.
Find them now in dreams
as your heads begin to nod.

On winter nights you'll dance
over moon-beam painted snow.
Now it's time for sleeping
while I rock you to and fro.

Tomorrow there'll be clover.
There'll be frolics in the grass.
Now sleep, darling bunnies,
until the night shall pass.

Father Beaver's Song

e still, my child, and listen to
the lap, lap, shu, shu
of the water all around.
Hear the gentle water's sound.

We felled the slender birch,
and floated logs across the pond.
We piled branches high
until each new day dawned.
Each night we started in anew,
weaving twigs and grass,
patching holes with mud
as rushing water tried to pass.

The dam grew, the pond rose.
Side by side we worked to make it so.
Your mother and your sister, too.
We built the dam and this lodge for you.
Be still, child, listen to
the lap, lap, shu, shu, lap, lap, shu.

The Mouse Lament

Baby mice, baby mice.
Count them once.
Count them twice.
There must be more
than three or four.
There could be ten,
but, then again
how could I know?
They've crowded me so.
There's no room to see.
There's no room for me!
Baby mice, baby mice.
Count them once.
Count them twice.
There are so, so many
Baby mice!

The Hedgehog's Song

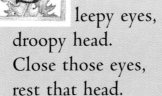

Sleepy eyes,
droopy head.
Close those eyes,
rest that head.

Sleep, baby hedgehog,
the sun grows bright.
Sleep, baby hedgehog,
surrender the night.

Soft, stubby quills,
curled up toes—
my precious one,
my briar rose.

Sleep, baby hedgehog,
the sun grows bright.
Sleep, baby hedgehog,
surrender the night.

The Stag's Song

awn lies alone near the glade
sleeping in the sun-splashed shade,
while Doe and I stand by.
But Fawn is kept from harm
by the Maker's clever charm.

For He has dappled Fawn with sunlight
to fool the hunter's eye.
And He has kept Fawn scentless
so danger will pass by.

Sleep on, my Fawn,
sleep soundly on.
Sweet child of the Woodland
held safely in His hand.

Dusk

When evening drapes the forest
or when the dawn draws nigh,
it is time for Woodland babies
to close their sleepy eyes.

Precious ones throughout the Woodland
in burrow, den and nest,
it is time to go to sleep
and let your parents rest.

About the Animal Babies

Red fox cubs are born without any markings. They are dark chocolate brown with bright pink noses. The mother vixen is colored a brilliant red, black, and white.

Baby moles are born in special nursery nests deep in the network of mother mole's tunnels. The grass and fur-lined nests are shaped like hollow footballs.

Owlets are completely helpless at birth. It takes many weeks before they can fly, and many more before they can feed themselves. Often owl families will stay together for a full year before the young set off on their own.

Bears are not true hibernators, like woodchucks, hamsters, and hedgehogs, although they do doze through much of the winter. Mother bears, called sows, give birth to one or two cubs. Babies are usually born in January or February, sometimes to a sleeping mother bear.

Bunnies are born during spring and summer in a hidden burrow. The doe visits her young once each night to nurse them. When she leaves, she covers the entrance to the burrow to keep her family safe and warm. In midwinter, rabbits sometimes do midnight dances on the hard crust of snow.

Beaver siblings will help mother and father beaver enlarge their lodge or build another to make room for a new litter of beaver kits.

Harvest mice weave grass and twigs into a hollow, round nursery nest, and line it with soft moss and thistledown. Five to eight babies are a normal-sized litter, but sometimes as many as twelve babies are born.

Hedgehogs, like many other animals of the woodland, are nocturnal. Active at night, they sleep through the day. Baby hedgehogs are naked at birth. Their quills don't appear for four or five days.

The doe watches over her fawn from a distance. When it lies still the fawn's spotted coat blends in with the sun-dappled ground. Fawns have no scent. Alone in the woodland with little cover, their invisibility and lack of odor keep them safe from predators.